Today Time Stands Still

By
Steven J. Newton, Sr.

Steven J. Newton, Sr.

Editor in Chief: Christian S. Newton

B.S in Criminal Justice

M.S in Adult, Occupation & Continuing Education

Managing Director: Jermario Jefferson

B.S. Criminal Justice Administration

Project Manager: Dione C. Simmons

B.S. Biological Science

M.S. in Psychology, Leadership Coaching

Book Cover Design: TKCG Information & Graphic Design Department

This document is copyrighted and protected by all applicable laws. This document and the accompanying audios may be redistributed as a whole only without change or alteration. Reproduction or distribution of this document in part is strictly forbidden unless the author prior gives permission.

© 2014 Steven J. Newton Sr. www.SJNSR.com

ISBN-13: 978-0-692-99409-2

CONTENTS

The Privilege of Now	1
Equivalence	8
The Value of Now	20
Today is a Reality	28
Tomorrow is Now	40
Today is Ultimate	49

About the Author

THE PRIVILEGE OF NOW

Dr. Martin Luther King spoke of the "fierce urgency of now." President Barack Obama echoed that statement in one of his speeches regarding universal healthcare. While I subscribe to the statement and believe that there is a tremendous urgency, my attempt is to share that NOW is urgent because NOW is all we have. God has given us the privilege of this very moment. It is at this very moment that time stands still. When we begin to walk in NOW we feel the very essence of God permeating through our very veins. Our DNA has no time connected to it. What a privilege to live in time but not be consumed with time. What a great responsibility however, to have to be accountable for the time that has been spent on this earth.

What if we didn't rush? What if there was no need to rush? To answer those questions we would have to dive into the thought of, why do we rush to begin with? In an act of rushing, we are moving in a rapid progression. Some even say when we rush we are violently progressing. Should we be violently progressing? Should life be so fast until we haven't noticed that we have lived. Everything around you is moving, most are giving no attention to anything going on around them. Are you in that picture? Are you on auto-pilot? Just letting life pass you by. Are you driver in your life or are you a spectator? Guess what, there is only one life you have to live which means you ONLY get to drive once. Letting someone else drive could cause major danger. Either they will have you in yesterday which is moving too slow or they will have you in tomorrow, which is moving too fast, and you need to be enjoying TODAY! Today is just right. If you are reading this book, you have today and that's enough to make a world of a difference. Many want to think about the flowers of tomorrow and that's okay; you must however, plant some seeds today or you can stop looking for flowers tomorrow. If you are looking for flowers tomorrow without planting seeds today, the only flowers you will have are those that belong to someone else. So tomorrow won't belong to you at all. You will ONLY get to share in someone else's today. Take charge of your today! Emily Dickinson an American poet who, despite the fact that less than a dozen of her nearly eighteen hundred poems were published during her lifetime, made a statement that really got me to thinking. She said, "forever is composed of nows." If you think about, that is very powerful. Especially coming from someone who is now considered one of the most original and influential poets of the 19th century. She wasn't thinking about the influence she might have as a result of her writing. She wrote about what she was feeling at that moment. It was her cuddle with the moment that was present before her that led to her being remembered forever. Her now, which didn't seem so significant, gained her notoriety in the world of poetry forever. Embracing this very moment that you have takes you out of time as normal. Your success tomorrow is literally bottled up into what you do right now. Today! Waiting is not an option. You will never recover this moment again. This is why right now is such a privilege. Knowing the gift you have in this current moment allows you to appreciate it more. You look for the opportunities that present itself in the moment instead of the problems the moment may expose.

One of the definitions of privilege is immunity. I love it! Since now is a privilege, that means I have been granted immunity from my past. WoW! This makes my future look very promising and makes me look at my present much differently. Knowing that my present moment doesn't have to influenced by my past is one of the most wonderful feelings, we can have as a human being. Our past could be absolutely insane, and unhinged from anything a normal person could fathom, but... yep, it's zeroed out. See whenever you use the word but in a sentence, it zeros or erases everything that was said before it. I have a past, but...

You're beautiful, but… Get the picture? Anything after that but is going to kill what was said before it. So go ahead now and write out all the reasons you don't think you could move forward and experience success beyond your wildest dreams and then under the list write BUT. Yep, but I have immunity. Now I am a citizen of the kingdom of God. I'm a Christian by lifestyle and not religion. I adhere to the principles Christ followed in the earth. Most that many people who say they follow him have no idea about. However, I believe in the finished work of the cross that we believe Jesus died on. As a result to the blood that was shed on that cross, we all have immunity. This is worth shouting over in every moment that presents itself. I can walk into every moment, every NOW knowing that it isn't influenced by my past. That is what makes today such an awesome day, everyday. Everyday is full of a different moment. Today I will get to experience a lot of nows. Every now activates another privileged opportunity to take the limitations off and get involved with potential greatness. What an honor that is from the God; the Creator of the universe.

EQUIVALENCE

When your dream becomes a reality, time no longer matters. However, over time we have come to the understanding that all things are not equal. No matter how you slice the piece of pie, there can never be any perfect parts. I recall slicing a piece of sweet potato pie once for my children after a Thanksgiving meal. They waited patiently for their fair share of the pie. As the aroma filled the room, their mouths watered with anticipation of the first bite. Unfortunately, the calmness of the moment turned into a major battle as the pieces were obviously cut into different proportions. Please bear with me as I explain. I obviously had no intentions on cutting the pie into different sizes for the others.

As I pondered on the lesson of equality during that scene from that moment in time, I paused to consider the distance between time and space. I'm considered a child from the era of the 80's. During this era, time seemed to move awfully slowly as compared to the age we are in presently. Sometimes when the mortgage, car notes, cable and utility bills roll in, I wish I could somehow slide back into that moment. During that time it just seemed like the time to be adult would never come. It seemed rather slow. As an adult with children of my own, I seem to have a struggle. Because to our current generation of millennials, "now" usually means "right now" to most of us. However the understanding of "nowness" can get caught up in a cloud with shades of grey, depending on the receiver or the giver of time. Like get off the phone now. Iron the clothes now. Turn the game off now. Get out of the bed now; it's time for church. Some sort of way my children's now is not my now. Consider standing in a long line at the grocery store, and notice how many people glance at their watches almost on cue every so many minutes to assure the person currently at the check out counter is on point and moving at the speed of a lightning. It is during this time, especially on a Sunday after church, when you're in Wal-Mart and they only have 4 of 19 aisles available for check out, that you think of all the things you could have been doing with your time, yet you're standing in this ridiculous line. That woman knew she was coming to Wal-Mart before she got here. She could have had some of that check already filled out. LOL I'm sure I'm not the only one.

Unfortunately for the majority of us, there is no equality in now. What exactly are we responsible for when it comes to time? The Bible states emphatically in *Hebrews Chapter 11 verse 1, Now faith is the substance of things hoped for and the evidence of things not seen.* So what I gather from that scripture is that we must have faith NOW. At this very moment in time, whatever we have hoped for must manifest in the essence of now because anything short of now mentioned in the previous scripture is totally outside of God's timing. Which brings me to this point. God's timing is emphatically and indisputably not on our time schedule. One day is as a THOUSAND years to the Lord. Psalms 90:4 in the Kings James version of scripture for you Bible readers. Now you do the math on that.

Time equality is not in texture of what we should be expecting in any walk of life, especially when dealing with others. What I may be able to accomplish in twenty-four hours may be different from you. While we have an equal amount of twenty-four hours, we do not share the same outlook on time, YET. Now is on a time level of frequency by itself. The ability to reduce the understanding of NOW to the lowest denominator cannot assist in the understanding to the purest frequency quota to God. I can state with an absolute resolve that God expects us to operate in the conduciveness of NOW. As we operate by going on and about with our regular activities, God is standing in a place and time zone called NOW. Do you dare join Him? Or do you continue to wonder about aimlessly as He continues to move on to the Omega of your triumph while you stand stagnant aimlessly in the Alpha of your test?

There is a song that is sweet to hear, but it just really makes my soul itch. The song says, "I don't mind waiting on the Lord." Excuse me while I wait on God! God is always in the NOW! So if you're waiting, it's NOT on God. Are you living in the past, present or future? If your answer is living in the past, you have just missed God in your assignment. Even if your answer may possibly be that you are living in the present, you just may find God isn't there either. The place called NOW where God has always resided is not a figment of your imagination. Please understand, if you plan on doing anything for God in this moment in time, God is always relevant; so you too must be relevant. God is always consistent and harmonious with now. Being relevant is always on God's mind. Certainly it does not have to take an act of Congress to get caught up in the relevance of Now!

Consider the beautiful models cladly dressed as they strut and sashay up and down the runway during high fashion week in the beautiful city of Paris. I got to see a little of this watching Tyra Bank's America's Next Top Model with my wife. I guess I can put up with it, if she can sit through House with me. LOL. In this show, perhaps there may be hundreds of models in the room, but only a handful will ever get noticed by the international press in order to become a household name. High fashion, on-point pictures, up to the minute updates, and experience in the field of modeling, will get the most nods at the end of the day. Remaining up to date and relevant matters to God, and relevance matters to those around you in everyday life.

A theory is that time and space are intricately linked and so connected that there may not be a particular time for everything. In other words, there is no set clock in space, but on the earth keeping time is highly important in order to meet the demands of commitment on a day to day basis. Astronauts in outer space can relate highly to this theory because when they are in the aircraft out in space, they may lose track of time if they did not have the space center gadgets to remind them of the time based on their soil in the USA or whatever country across the globe they reside. When you find the thing you are passionate about, you will understand this. This will be relevant to you, if it isn't already. When you find yourself shut off from the rest of the world, doing what you love, you forget what time it is here on earth. You are completely lost in space. Lost in love. Lost in creativity. Lost in TODAY!

The relevance of keeping time is a man made ideology. God never keeps time, because He is time and resides outside of time. As men and women in our earth suits, we recognize time because of the fact that we are growing older day by day. They hit the clock when you came into the world, and they will hit it when you leave. I've noticed the older I become, time becomes more relevant to me. As I appropriate the idea of living in the newness of nowness, I recognize the importance of both time zones: *Chronos* and *Kiaros*. They become highly relevant in my life due to the fact without knowing the difference and understanding how both time zones are relevant in my life, I may have failed with the Father for now. *Chronos* is measured with clocks and calendars. *Kairos* is God's timing; this time cannot be measured. This is the supreme moment when God intersects with our lives. *Kairos* is the moment when God's will happens. *Kairos* is when the right things happen in the right time.

In Greek mythology, *Chronos* means either time or year. The Greek god was said to have been basically a god of order. In saying this, as we continue to discuss the NOW factor. The Bible says a day is like a thousand years and a thousand years is like a day. This scripture is proof that God's time is not like our time. As He stands on the cusp of NOW, we should be joining him with an urgency that chances are we could miss opportunities if we are not available when the God-shift happens right in our midst.

Just imagine as you are sitting there reading these words, God is moving instantly on your behalf and unfortunately before I end this sentence, your NOW moment just came and went and you did not even recognize it as it exited. Leaving NOW, arriving NOW, producing NOW, creating NOW and most importantly dominating NOW. This is the relevance of NOW. You see how you feel right now, TIME JUST STOOD STILL!

THE VALUE OF NOW

Not every moment carries the same value. Every second of your day has a different value. Let's say for example, my mom has a birthday party going on at 2pm this afternoon, but the fellas that I hang with on the weekend have scheduled a basketball game on the court at 2pm. It's 2pm in both locations. However, the value of the smile on my mother's face when I walk into her party is worth more than the high-five or dap I will get from the fellas when I walk into the gym on the court. Same second; different value. I hope by now you are getting the power of TODAY.

There are 86,400 seconds in a day. If time is money, and it is, then my friend, welcome to the millionaires club! That's 31,536,000 seconds a year. WOW! The difference between you and other millionaires is simply what you do with those seconds. How do you value those seconds? The answer to that question makes the difference. How much value are you adding to others in those seconds? This is going to really open some eyes when it comes to time. Today just made you a millionaire. What is tomorrow going to make you? We don't know, which is why we aren't concerned with it. We just know what today made you. And what you do with what you have today will determine what you have tomorrow.

The good news is that God has given you a new day, everyday. While we may know now from our previous chapter that we are immune to our past, how about we make the past good enough to build from? Yes, we have immunity from our past, but what if our past wasn't so bad; what if it wasn't like a disease that we needed to seek immunity from? What if what we did with today was so productive that it helped to build a solid foundation for tomorrow? So now we can go to sleep tonight, excited about tomorrow because we know when we wake up, what was tomorrow has become today and today is better than it would have been because of what I did yesterday. That makes sleep time become true rest and relaxation. That permits our dreams to become the spa where our ideas hangout and get a good massage until it's time for them to be released in the earth. They are resting, and increasing in value by the day, as the need arises for it to be exhibited and amasses the wealth in the physical world as it did in the spiritual and mental world. As a result, we can explore from the physical manifestation and hanging out at the spa becomes our new spot. So we can go and get a massage until it time for us to be released back into the world to display even more of God's splendor. What a joy life becomes when we value now. To value is to consider with respect to worth, excellence, usefulness, or importance. We value what we believe! If we believe in the clock, we place our trust in what it shows us. Now time as a result of the clock operates only as a function of our belief. 24 hours in a day, seven days in a week, three hundred sixty five days in a year. Looks like we have to hurry and scurry along huh…

What if we understood that eternity was within each and every one of us? Would there be a need to be tardy? Would there be a need to be in a rush? Instead of trying to control time, what would happen if we took authority over ourselves? Instead of time management, we have "me" management. Your higher, more eternal self has a higher, more eternal schedule to keep. You are on assignment. You were sent to this earth with a purpose. You are on a universal timeline. Your conscious spirit knows there is a better timeline than the one that is predicated on humankind. We get to change it when we want. Daylight savings time was written in the mountains somewhere. Someone name George Vernon Hudson thought of that in 1895, and we as a people adopted it. This is the practice of advancing clocks during the lighter months so that evenings have more daylight and mornings have less. Typically clocks are adjusted forward one hour near the start of spring and are adjusted backward in the autumn. Your life can't be based on man-made adjustments. When you change your belief structure regarding time, you can change the value you give to it.

Daylight savings time was invented for the purpose of commercial production. It was a business proposal that was accepted globally. The difficulty with being bound by that is determined on what time zone you're in, determines your level of productivity. What would happen when you lived as eternity as your time zone? Instead of Central, Eastern, Mountain, Pacific, Atlantic, or Reunion zones, you place yourself on Eternity. That's amazing, I promise!

At the moment of release from the world's clock, and the jump to God's eternal clock, your limits change. Your deadlines and commitments function on universal time. Understand that time is only man's attempt to qualify and quantify its existence. When we choose to let go of the idea of being bound by time, we have much more of it to appreciate by being present to the greatness of the moment we find ourselves standing and with whom we are standing with.

Time has no holiday. There is no time to set aside and celebrate time. Time is a free force. You can't be bound by something that isn't bound. If you are connected to something that is free, hanging out with it long enough will set your free. Valued time reminds you to act and act wisely. Time is wise. It doesn't stay still and it never repeats itself. It holds no grudges. In our effort to be smart, we do things and refer to it as, "killing time." Time has us beat so much so until when you think about it, you're not killing time, you're committing suicide. It's your own life you're wasting and not time's life. Time can't be killed, only our dreams, goals, and aspirations. Time keeps going and comes to our funeral. You do know when you die, the funeral directors ask your family, what TIME would they prefer the service? So hey, you can fool yourself by thinking you're killing time, and it will be the main guest at your burial.

Time conquers all. That means anyone who is a friend to time, has the opportunity to conquer all. Why be friends with a winner and never learn to win. Don't complain about the winning and the fact it keeps winning. Join it, embrace it, and conquer with it! Become one with time, and you will be become one with winning all the time.

TODAY IS A REALITY

Nowadays reality television shows are on almost every channel as you flip from one to the other. The reality TV business seems to be around to stay for a while. These shows continue to increase in ratings simply because these producers have discovered their niche market. Today's niche markets are those people who love famous people. This is why one of the highest ranking reality shows, "Keeping Up With the Kardashians" remains at the top of the reality charts. But what is "reality" really, anyway?

Is reality an illusion or what? What is the frequency of NOW when it comes to reality? How does one face reality in this life? These are the questions that many of us would like to understand the answer to, but in most cases seem too complicated to answer. The raw meaning of reality is simply this: many of you live in an obscure place called there, when God wants to bring you into a oneness of NOW.

    Reality shows make it big on TV because they give viewers a false sense of awareness that is not reality at all. In fact the reality illusion is creating this false sense of materialistic ideologies and minute mindsets about life that creates a false sense of security about everyday life. However, take this same niche market and share the Gospel of NOW with them and they would not be able to comprehend this way of thinking. The Reality of Now is among us. Unfortunately many of us refuse to operate in this truth.

What is real time? I love it when I hear techies state information is happening in real time. If this is a matter of truth and determination then this real time is a good thing. However who's the best authority of real time anyway? In my most honest opinion, there is no better authority than God when it comes to real time. Now going back to our scripture in Hebrews 11:1, *Now faith is the substance of things hoped for and the evidence of things not seen.* Let's pause right here at the word "substance" because "The Reality of Now" falls right there in the word "substance".

The "substance" of things hoped for. Substance has a meaning that substantiates the obvious; substance is reality. Without having substance there would be no reality. The synonyms for the word substance sums up the phenomenon of the meaning beautifully: bona fide, genuine, and authentic. All of these words sum up the NOWness of the goodness of our God! I feel it within me and NOW I believe you may finally be catching on to the Reality of Now!

NOW can never be created by a producer of a television show. Unfortunately, God is the only orchestrator of NOW, but man has continued to try for ages to no avail. I totally understand the reason for trying because as time moves on, Gods creation becomes more and more impatient with the twenty-four hour clock man has to live by in the earth. While time keeps on ticking into the future, man grows more and more determined to either waste time or attempt to re-gain time in what's called the fountain of youth. The fountain of youth is an imaginary place that many have tried to place in a bottle of potions and creams that continue to earn millions of dollars. Speaking of this fountain of youth, many others gain access to reduce the aging process because they can afford to go through the expensive surgeries and treatments that seem to temporarily pull back the curtain of time.

To many, time is of the essence and must be created for a new reality for those who are willing to spend their life savings and last hard earned dollars on these expensive and many times useless products, surgeries and diets. The simplest way to understand the reality of now is to embrace the change that is coming your way. Time can become more predictable as we remain in the safe zone. The ONLY true safety we have is in NOW. Enjoy your now because that's what you have and even if you died within an hour of reading this book, you would have still died TODAY.

Most of us desire instant gratification. The reality of this is evident in almost every area of our lives. In every major city on the globe as far and wide, we see fast food restaurants on every corner in our societies as we begin to expect the fact that now is much better than next week. May I suggest another thought, perhaps we can have everything we want instantly and never have to wait again? As a matter of fact, God had it all in His plan from the beginning by requiring us to use what is called faith. Hebrews 11:1 states, *Now faith is the substance of things hoped for and the evidence of things not seen.* May I go even further to suggest a simple notion that the action of now can be quite simplistic if we place a dose of faith on the thing we are waiting for.

It's not necessary to have it your way Burger King style, fast and in a hurry, instantly and right now! Well is it? Of course not. But if you are a child of the Most High God, and you are, you can in fact have every desire in your wildest dreams, TODAY. I say this because it is possible to believe that everything you want or need is already yours and you already have it. Hoping alone is a time thief, but hope combined with faith is a promise kept. Hope establishes a contract with God that we trust Him, but faith seals the deal. We can have hope instantly, and in our hoping our waiting doesn't seem to be delayed. With faith there is no such thing as hope deferred. Hope deferred is not a part of the vocabulary of those of us who are pure in heart and in right standing with God.

Have you ever misplaced something of value to you and proceeded to look for the item hectically and sometimes furiously until finally giving up. Moreover, blaming others in your household for the loss of your property. Perhaps the item was a set of keys, your reading glasses or simply one lonely sock that happens to be out there in the universe where socks seem to disappear from time to time. I mean is it me or can you relate to putting matching socks in the laundry, you saw them hit the dryer and somehow when it's time to do the laundry, one got away? With these simple and sometimes complicated losses, there is nothing that is more aggravating than the loss of time. More precious than losing any of the items aforementioned, or any amount of money in the world, time lost is time wasted.

Today, right now, is not a place that we can see; instead it is an awareness of knowing what we desire is finally in our grip. Now is relative because the senses can never be satisfied by the time span of now. The saying "now is the time" is really superlative because time simply has nothing to do with now. What is now superlatively speaking: quickly, more quickly, most quickly? Are we able to have our desires met within one of these time zones, or is it possible to simply wait a little bit longer than quick? Can we have it quicker than quick, or is the presence of now simply a farce?

Many people today have this ideology, "I'd rather have the quick thing, than have to wait on God for a better time than now." This thinking is the reason we have such drama in our lives. The thought of, "Waiting on God" seems so cliche compared to the ideology of wanting time to wait on us.

Get rich quick schemes are being preached from the pulpit to the small chat rooms on online social networks. Becoming a millionaire mogul is the dream of most in this Now Generation that will be taking over in every arena: faith, religion, politics, market place, education and on and on. Don't be confused, I do not argue with those who wish to become millionaires. I am one, on my way to billionaire status. However, I will argue that real wealth grows over time and does not happen fast, quick and in a hurry, as these get rich quick gurus promise. Now is relational, so it is fitting for most to fall into these money-making traps. Unfortunately for the majority of those who join in these programs all they lose is their money and time. The evidence of time valued is the best approach to building wealth over time. Now is relational because time is a place "way down the road" for some. Waiting on God is the most rational approach, because God is out of time. Not only is God out of time, by the time we grasp hold of His initial instructions given, He is far ahead of us and has forged ahead to His next move.

    Time is unseen and this is one of the reasons God has given us Now Faith, because He has the foresight and the wisdom we lack in regards to time. Because He saw us in the beginning of time, He assumed a position of authority in our future. Knowing this is why time is so simplistic because in knowing where we are in God (out of time), we begin to know that waiting, for us (His children), becomes a non-factor. Let's revisit Hebrews 11:1 again, "the evidence of things unseen or not seen". Again time is not seen as far as man is concerned because it is impossible to wrap our minds around the essence of time.

TOMORROW IS NOW

The last chapter was titled Today is Reality and this chapter is simply, Tomorrow is Now. Tomorrow absolutely NEVER seems to get here. Waiting on tomorrow will trick you. As soon as your so-called friend, tomorrow, gets here to help you, it's today. Once upon a time in the days of old, there was a group of people who decided to build a tower to reach heaven. God said, if you will allow me to paraphrase, if these people remain with one mindset, they are capable of anything. You see once we maintain solidarity in our thinking, nothing or no-one can stop us, not even time. Once we come into union with today and separate ourselves from the thought of being time bound creatures, IT ONLY GETS BETTER! The process of getting everything together is basically all you need to get any project done. Once the concept is developed, time is no longer an issue, because the project comes to life at the very moment the idea comes out of your imagination and is distributed among the other players in a particular group or tribe, so to speak.

The moment in time that solidarity or agreement occurs, is when the idea takes feet and runs like a blazing wildfire consuming everything that is in it's path if not directed properly or eventually quenched. It is for this one concept alone that God knew the idea of solidarity was very good, but the magnitude of delivery would be the problem at hand. Man loves immediate gratification and this is the moment sin crept into the plans of the tower builders.

What they thought was a great idea, and would be pleasing to God, was merely a plan with a hidden agenda. God in His essence of time and remaining out of time was able to see the problem way ahead of the bad idea and quench that wildfire before one spark could fester a blaze.

The Tower of Babel is a supreme example of both the danger of solidarity and the beauty of the dynamics of the thought of being on one accord. The human mind is often evil to the core if the person behind the thinking lacks a consciousness of God. The only way to really know how God thinks is to read His word and be in His presence. Then you must separate yourself from the idea of ever being separated from God to begin with. Once there is a disconnect one way or another, sin will come knocking at the door of your sub-consciousness where ideas, methods, theologies, religious rituals, consuming negative thoughts, judgements and your core values lie dormant until an idea is formed. Once the idea forms whether good or bad, right or wrong, occurs within your psyche, your subconsciousness will be the first line of response. Failure to analyze or process the idea allows sin to have its way and ruin what once was a good idea. Sin is simply to miss the mark. To miss your mark is to miss your assignment. To miss your assignment is to miss time. To miss time is sin. The sin is not just what you were doing at the time you were "sinning," it's what you could have done in line with your assignment and you misappropriated that time.

Now is the time to process ideas through prayer and fasting more than ever before, because depending on where the idea comes from determines the root intentions of it down to the minute details. With most wanting to just initiate a response, right now, we may lose the time we have by jumping on an idea that was not sent from the throne room of His presence. Here is another example of what I am talking about. Do you remember the last bad idea you engaged in? Perhaps it was a multilevel marketing program or the purchase of a bad automobile that turned out to be a lemon. Both ideas when presented looked good on the surface, nice, shiny and brand new; but underneath the surface was more than your wallet or time could handle. So ask yourself the question, was it worth your time? If you are honest with yourself, no it wasn't at all.

Salespeople are most cunning at getting us in a position to make a purchase by compelling us with sales tactics that they practice everyday. Everyone by now knows most people are compulsive buyers. Salespeople often play off of this knowledge and understanding of the consumer. Consumers are the bottom feeders of our economy, but please don't take this statement personal. Bear with me as I explain. Consumers will spend even in a slow economy because there is something about spending that fulfills their desire. Much is to be said about instant gratification, having to have it all now, even though that brand new shiny object in the window is not in the family budget. But somehow, now grabs the consumer by the neck and drags them to the check out line in order to make a purchase that is not affordable or not needed.

Since God spends His time, outside of time, unfortunately, He occasionally must step into our time in order to clean up our mess because we have to have our desires met instantly, which often causes us to get into troubles. But God in His sovereignty will step in and fix the situation in record time, just when we need Him. However, on some occasions God warns us to wait. Now waiting can be the most difficult for God's people depending on their level of maturity. God will allow things to happen on our timetable just as a reminder that He is relational and is always there. But He also has to test us to prove that we are able to handle that thing we are asking for. He looks on lovingly as we cringe with anxiety and fear, thinking

He may never show up on our behalf, but if we realized He is, the God who is always there, then we would not fall into the trap of fear. Fear causes us to wait even longer because fear is sin, and God can never be where sin is. Remember God is, and that should be enough to comfort you on whatever level you are waiting on. Sin is simply to miss the mark. To miss your mark is to miss your assignment. To miss your assignment is to miss time. To miss time is to miss God.

God is always there. There is a saying, "He may not come when you want Him to, but He is always on time." Honestly, if you really knew God, then you would know by now this is not a true statement of God's character. The character of God is in direct enmity with any suggestive character flaw of man.

Since God is definitely out of our time, then the statement above would suggest God is late. Therefore understanding God is never late, then how could he possibly be on time? As a matter of fact the error in repeating an untrue statement about God is borderline blasphemy. Let's think clearly through ideas, thoughts and statements thoroughly before repeating them. The finality of God declares His timeliness in our problems. The "isness" of God denotes He is always answering our prayers. The essence of God declares His ongoing presence in our situations, and the fragrance of God declares His entrance into our worship. God is…time that stands still…is forever moving forward and even backed up when necessary. God is time redeemed. God's approach to now is always present tense. Enjoy today!

Today is Ultimate

As the Bride frantically prepares for her Groom, the wedding guest are growing more impatient as the clock ticks forward. The sound of the clock's pendulum moves backwards and forward in a synchronized symphony of sound that often deafens the ears of the most attentive causing the guest to constantly gaze at their timepieces almost in unison. The crowd begins to grow more impatient, the sound of sighing and shushing of fidgeting children grow louder and louder. Finally, a distinct muffled, but dignified voice comes across the sound system to awaken the ears of the once patient but now irritated crowd and says, "the wedding ceremony is about to begin now!" The voice that once began in a slow muffle began to grow into a loud bellow as music begins to play. The lively sound of horns, drums, flutes, guitars and a piano suddenly began to permeate the entire room tickling the itching ears of guest who had previously been anxious for nothing.

This exact scene is played out in houses of worship across the nation on any given Sunday. But instead of a wedding march being played, a variety of worship music takes it's place, and instead of the bride frantically getting ready for her groom, the music department will perform and the worshipers will be ushered in and on cue prompted to sing along. Everything from this point on is strategically planned and strategically timed. Again time in the hands of man is of no value compared to time left in the hands of God. If we allowed God to show up in our houses of worship more often than not, this rat race we call life filled with rushing, hustle and bustle would be unnecessary at best. The I Am that I Am provides His presence and from the beginning of a thing to the finality of a thing, there would be no explanation for anything except that all of our desires would inevitably be met in a timeless space called Now.

Once time is lost, reliving time is irrevocable. If the timeliness of now is irreplaceable, once passed by there is no point of return; why on earth do we try to push and shove, rushing through, often running over to get to somewhere we've been before. We rush from one worship service to the next, one job to the next, from one class to the next, and ultimately we run out of steam trying to get every task done quick, fast and in a hurry. We rush through life at the speed of sound, forgetting the speed of light is so much faster. Light is certainly quicker than sound, as is God's timing the totality of now. His timing is the final word. His is the final yes to all of our questions of why, when, how, where and why not right now?

The end is near as we await the sound of the trumpet of the archangel Gabriel and as many of us end time radicals await this upcoming moment in time with much anticipation. Seemingly Christians have been waiting for centuries for this particular day to arrive, but only God knows the day and hour when this event will occur. I mention this because as we anticipate this happening anytime now, we must also understand the meaning of waiting on God and the finality of time. How much longer will we wait, I really cannot answer this question. But what I will attempt to remind you of is God is all knowing and all powerful which is reason enough to remain in His presence and bask in the glory of now with Him always.

The conclusion we must all come to know in regards to the matter of time, is that time continues to manifest with or without us. Being rushed or hurried in our business does not give time an expiration date, so why not take your time and enjoy life now. Please understand I am not speaking of ignoring the sense of urgency or becoming happy-go-lucky forgetting all rules and responsibilities. However, the urgency we should adopt is that of a steward, and create our own inner urgency to exist and appreciate the time we do have before us. When we do this, we begin to operate within the timing of our Creator who is never late. but always repeatedly responsive to our timetable, as well as understanding our appetite for fast action in a fast paced society. Again, let's not take advantage of His Goodness, but instead tune into His own respect of time where each of us is concerned with full understanding He is always there, now. Today!

Finally, as we continue to forge ahead in our lives by pushing our ways into the atmosphere of others whether knowingly or unknowingly, we fight a battle with the principalities and powers of the air that never sleep. In our universe there is always movement, and perhaps this is the most intriguing misunderstanding of human kind. We love movement and we love to have a sense of urgency in order to feel as if we are getting things done. In our quest to avoid time dominators and thieves we seem to have misplaced the logic of the finality of time. Time has no beginning, nor does it have an ending, so what in the world can we expect now? After all, now is actually an unknown location that we recklessly pursue haphazardly without any realization that now may not ever come. Nevertheless, we continue to pursue that place called Now with confident feeling in our inner core that we will be fulfilled and this fulfillment is our success.

So before you run another red light, or cut someone else off in traffic; ask yourself is that few seconds that could cause a terrible accident worth loosing today? Is that moment in the argument with a spouse that could end in tragedy worth losing today? Is that moment of anger with a child, worth loosing today? Today is all we will ever have, and hopefully, you choose to LOVE today.

ABOUT THE AUTHOR

When you hear terms like creative, expressive, innovative and enterprising; you think of Apostle Steven J. Newton Sr., intimately known as "Apostle Steve." Apostle Steve is the President/CEO at The Kingdom Center Global, a global church planting network founded by he and his wife, Christian. Apostle Steven J. Newton Sr. is a celebrated leader of many around the world. Until now, only a fortunate few have been able to draw from the water that God has placed inside of this "well." As God has placed many leading men and women of God in the earth, there is absolutely no substitute for Apostle Steve.

Apostle Steve teaches with an approach of capability without complexity. His ability to tap into the heavens and withdraw spontaneous, pulse-pounding, incisive revelation from God is provocative. The illustrations and information that Apostle Steve uses to coach over 120,000 people all over the globe to the next level in life seem to be organically grown in the Garden of Eden. To sit at the feet of one of such five-star quality of excellence is a pleasurable feast and quite adventurous.

With over 25 years of ministry experience, Apostle Steve's elegant yet practical gift to compel others to live and experience God's best for their lives are far beyond his age. Being groomed for success by many distinguished and well-respected men and women of God across denominational and religious lines, allows him to be an effective communicator in various facets of life. From marriage and family to government and media, Apostle Steven J. Newton Sr., was endowed with a "can't miss" anointing that if the listener follows through with what is heard, results are inevitable.

Apostle Steven J. Newton Sr. has four children, Jer'miya (ladybug) Steven Jr. (tiger), Jamichael (pig), and Victoria (butterfly) and is happily married to his teammate and most wonderful friend, Pastor Christian Newton (formerly Jones) and he lives in Shreveport, LA.

www.ingramcontent.com/pod-product-compliance
Lightning Source LLC
Chambersburg PA
CBHW070134100426
42744CB00009B/1837